Does God Exist,

And Has He Spoken to Us?

Bob Evely

To

Our amazing grandchildren,

Ten thus far.

You bring so much joy into our lives,

And we cherish every moment we have together.

May God bless you beyond measure,

All the days of your lives!

With love,

Grampa & Grandma

Does God Exist

And Has He Spoken to Us?

A Consideration of the Evidence

Bob Evely.

Copyright 2021, Robert W. Evely, Wilmore KY

*Scriptures taken from the Concordant Literal New Testament
and the Concordant Version of the Old Testament unless otherwise noted.
Concordant Publishing Concern, P O Box 449, Almont, MI 48003
Concordant.org*

P O Box 6, Wilmore, KY 40390
GraceEvangel.org

Writings; Does God Exist, and Has He Spoken to Us?
by Bob Evely
Copyright © 2021 by Robert W. Evely

First Printing: 2021

ISBN 978-1-7323228-5-1

Cover created by Cris Evely
Front: Photo by Molly Evely, taken at the Evely farm in Kentucky
  (MollyEvelyPhotography.com)
Back: Photo by Jill Evely, taken at the Evely farm in Kentucky

Published by:
Robert W. Evely
P.O. Box 6
Wilmore, KY 40390

GraceEvangel.org

Table of Contents

Opening Remarks

One hundred years ago a preacher could hold his Bible up and proclaim, "This is the word of the Lord." And those hearing this proclamation believed it to be so without question. But skepticism has grown. Men and women have become less concerned with the spiritual things of God, and more concerned with living life in the material world. The Bible no longer commands the respect it once did. It is no longer deemed to be an authority or a guide to life.

At the beginning of Chapter 1 of his excellent book, "God's Eonian Purpose" (1929), Adlai Loudy states the importance of considering this matter as follows:

> *"Are the Scriptures of God or man? is a question uppermost in many honest hearts today. In other words, Did God write them, or are they simply a collection of the writings of men? If they are simply a collection of man's writings, without divine guidance, then they are no more reliable than fallible man. But if God wrote them, they must be true and we can depend on their admonitions and teachings, prophecies, and promises."*

There are still many believers in God, and in Christ, and in the Bible; but they are not equipped to explain to others why THEY should believe. The argument is, at times, "because the Bible says it is so." But why should those throughout the world believe the Bible is legitimate? Today's believer is not equipped to answer this question. And that is the reason I am writing this book.

Many today talk about the immortality of mankind, and they espouse their beliefs about what happens once this life has ended. But what makes us think we are immortal? Do we base this on wishful thinking, human reasoning, or perhaps the philosophers of old?

Death is inescapable. We will all face death at some point. The question is — on what will we depend regarding that which will happen *after* death?

I contend that when this life is over there will be *nothing* we can depend upon other than God. He created all things including life itself, and it is *He* Who decides what will happen next. And since I believe the Bible is God's revealed word to us (as I will substantiate in the remainder of this work), I contend that God will raise us from the dead and *make* us immortal at the time of His choosing; and not before. I contend that while the resurrection of Jesus was a supernatural, historic event — it is in fact much more than that! It was a demonstration of God's plan for all of us. But we can depend only upon Him to make this happen.

But this is certainly far better than relying upon human reasoning, or wishful thinking, or the speculations of a philosopher. God created! And He will carry out His plans in full for His creation!

I believe the Bible is God's revealed word to mankind; and my purpose in writing here is to explain WHY I believe this to be so.

This is not intended to be a scholarly thesis. I want to present the evidence at a high level in such a way to get my reader's attention, causing them to contemplate the basic thoughts I will share, and to dig deeper with further reading if they wish to learn more. (And I sincerely hope this does happen!)

While some of the thoughts I will share are original, much has been culled from a variety of sources. The book I started with and from which many of my points were derived is "The New Evidence that Demands a Verdict" by Josh McDowell. I will not for the most part quote specific references from this book, nor the sources quoted by McDowell in producing his book. I will simply say to you – if you want to dig deeper into any of the points I make, start with McDowell's excellent book. It is an encyclopedia of evidence supporting the conclusion that God is the Creator of this world and universe, and that the Bible is His revelation to mankind.

Upon revisiting McDowell's book many years after my initial reading, I supplemented by digging through other books on my shelves. I provide references to these sources along the way so you can examine them for yourself. One in particular that I highly recommend is "Who Moved the Stone?" by Frank Morison. The author was a journalist who set out to disprove the resurrection accounts found in the Bible but found that upon closer scrutiny these accounts rang true as accurate historical accounts. This book is very engaging and is most worthy of the reader's time.

My objective, then, is to stay high level in this overview, simply pointing you to the many pieces of evidence that I have considered and that have shaped my understanding of God, His creation, and how He has chosen to communicate with mankind.

Some will have objections before we begin an objective view of things. Why? Because they will not want to even consider there MIGHT be *objective, absolute truth* that would impose moral values or condemn certain behaviors in any way. They will not want to believe there is a God, and that He has certain absolutes built into His created order or into any written revelations that originated with Him. They might go so far as to say that all truth is relative, and what is true for one may not be true for another.

But when it comes to historical truth, things either happened or they did not. Jesus either existed, or he did not. He was either resurrected from the dead, or He was not. The Bible has been passed down through the ages in reliable form, or it was not. God has either used men and women to preserve His revelation and pass it down to us, or He has not. We can only seek to discover that which is, in fact, the truth.

And if there is a Creator, and if He created the universe, and if He made certain revelations to mankind that He would like for us to know, and if He has a purpose in His creation, and if there is a blueprint that will guide us along life's path – then we can either objectively examine the evidence available to us to reach our conclusions about these things, or we can turn away.

Hopefully with issues of this magnitude and that possibly have such great bearing upon our lives, we will choose the former.

And as for critics of God and anything spiritual, as Gilbert West says in "A Defense of the Christian Revelation," – *Whoever has either neglected or refused to make this examination can have no right to pass his judgment upon Christianity.*

So let us begin our journey in considering the evidence set before us.

Does God Exist?

———

If God exists, we can know of His existence even if He chose not to reveal Himself *directly* and more *specifically*.

The house that I live in was built long ago. I have never met the builder and am sure he is dead by now. I have no written communication from him. I have only this house that he once built.

Yet I know that the builder *existed* because of the visible evidence of what he once did. And I can infer a few specifics about him. I know he was skilled in certain ways to be able to build a home like this ... with complicated roof lines, a brick coal fireplace, and some moldings and trim that are a step above the bare basics. The existence of this house is a fact. Its characteristics that can be examined reveal to me that there was a builder responsible for its construction — along with some degree of information about the builder.

So also the world and the observable universe are realities that can be examined, and evidence of a Creator.

Not only can we see that a Creator existed, but by studying and contemplating the visible creation we can draw a few conclusions about the Creator. The Creator is *wise*, having built into the universe much intricate detail. Everything seems to fit and work together in harmony. The Creator is *mighty*, having the *ability* to bring this massive vision into existence. Where would we begin if we chose to undertake so great a task? And the Creator is *creative*, as is evidenced by the beauty of the mountains, the rivers, the trees, and the many varieties of plants and flowers and birds.

So without having any further communication with mankind, God's fingerprint is all around us, and it reveals to us information about this wise, mighty, powerful Creator.

Stand back objectively without any preconceived notion of God's existence. Look closely at the world around you. Consider how interrelated things are!

In "Why I Believe," D. James Kennedy summarizes the mathematical evidence in support of a wise Creator. When one examines the universe (as much of it as we can examine) it seems to be one gigantic thought of a great mathematician. It is well ordered and symmetrical. Furthermore the earth is of a precise size to support life. It is just the right distance from the sun. The tilt of the earth's axis provides a moderation of temperature to support life. The moon is the right size and distance from the earth to provide the tides which not only cleanse our shores but also aerate the oceans to provide for plankton which is essential to the foundation of our food chain. The mix of nitrogen and oxygen in the air is the correct balance to support life. Water provides many essential functions within the earth and within our bodies. And so on. I recommend reading Mr. Kennedy's entire book as it provides many other great details the reader will find fascinating and thought-provoking. (Though I disagree with his beliefs concerning the Bible's teachings on heaven and hell, and provide evidence concerning the correct Biblical understanding in my own book, "At the End of the Ages, the Abolition of Hell.")

Another excellent little book that would be well worth your time is "So You Don't Believe in God?" by Russell V. DeLong. The author provides some great detail on the following categories of evidence in support of God's existence.

1. The favorable distance of the sun from the earth.
2. The rotation of the earth on its axis.
3. The earth's 365-day orbit combined with its axis.
4. The pull of the moon upon the earth.
5. The fixed orbits of the planets.
6. The precise percentage of oxygen in the atmosphere.

7. The correct air pressure upon our bodies.
8. The existence of life and its transmission.
9. The exchange of oxygen and carbon dioxide between plants and animals.
10. The genes which control hereditary characteristics.
11. The incredible circulatory system within our bodies.
12. The intricate structure of the human eye.
13. The uniqueness of our intelligence and ability to reason.

Consider the intricacies of our human bodies and what a wonder they are! Consider how precisely the human body is constructed. Consider the many parts of the body – the variety, how each part has its purpose, the dependence of one part to the others, the brain as its command center. Consider the ability to reason, to think, to make decisions, to mobilize the various part of the body to act at the beckoned call of the brain. Consider the intricacies of the human eye and how it works in conjunction with the brain and enables us to have vision. Consider the specific, detailed structure of DNA, or the thousands of amino acids working together within every human cell (some say there are 200,000).

Consider life itself! Mankind can create to some degree (art, music, literature) but nothing like the multifaceted, animated, thinking, breathing, living creature that we are!

It's hard to fathom this all could have occurred spontaneously without the work of a Creator. Throughout all of biology, intelligent causes are necessary to explain the complex structures.

I suggest that an examination and contemplation of this world and universe tells us *clearly* that there was a Creator behind all of this; an intelligent, wise, powerful Creator.

If you happen upon a smartphone laying on the sidewalk, and as you examine it, would you believe such a complex device could have possibly come into existence spontaneously – without a designer and manufacturer behind it? Or would you deduce there was some intelligent designer responsible?

It seems ludicrous to conclude that this smart phone, or this home in which I live, suddenly appeared spontaneously without a designer, manufacturer, or builder behind it. Likewise it seems ludicrous to conclude that this world and universe, and these bodies animated by life, came into existence without there being a creator involved.

Testimony from a former atheist

I highly recommend "There Is a God" by Antony Flew, an outspoken atheist who came to believe there is a God. Following are just a few snippets from this book.

When asked in 2004 if recent work on the origin of life pointed to the activity of a creative intelligence, Flew replied: "Yes, I now think it does … almost entirely because of the DNA investigations. What I think the DNA material has done is that it has shown, by the almost unbelievable complexity of the arrangements which are needed to produce [life], that intelligence must have been involved in getting these extraordinarily diverse elements to work together. It's the enormous complexity of the number of elements and the enormous subtlety of the ways that they work together." (p. 75)

"I now believe that the universe was brought into existence by an infinite intelligence. I believe that this universe's intricate laws manifest what scientists have called the Mind of God. I believe that life and reproduction originate in a divine Source." (p. 88)

"Science spotlights three dimensions of nature that point to God …
- Nature obeys laws.
- The dimension of life, of intelligently organized and purpose-driven beings, which arose from matter.
- The very existence of nature …" (p. 88)

"The important point is not merely that there are regularities in nature, but that these regularities are mathematically precise, universal, and 'tied together.' Einstein spoke of them as 'reason incarnate.' The question we should ask is how nature came packaged in this fashion." (p. 96)

Flew shares a thought from Oxford philosopher John Foster: "If you accept the fact that there are laws, then something must impose that regularity on the universe. What agent (or agents) brings this about?" (p. 110)

And from physicist Freeman Dyson, "The more I examine the universe and study the details of its architecture, the more evidence I find that the universe in some sense knew we were coming." Flew adds, "In other words, the laws of nature seem to have been crafted so as to move the universe toward the emergence and sustenance of life." (p. 114)

"How can a universe of mindless matter produce beings with intrinsic ends, self-replication capabilities, and coded chemistry?" (p. 124)

Flew shares a challenge from David Conway in responding to David Hume's atheistic contention: "The first challenge is to produce a materialistic explanation for the very first emergence of living matter from non-living matter. ... The second challenge is to produce an equally materialistic explanation for the emergence, from the very earliest life-forms which were incapable of reproducing themselves, to life-forms with a capacity for reproducing themselves." (p. 125)

A word from scientist Gerald Schroeder: "The existence of conditions favorable to life still does not explain how life itself originated. Life was able to survive only because of favorable conditions on our planet. But there is no law of nature that instructs matter to produce end-directed, self-replicating entities." (p. 131)

Mankind's desire to elevate himself

Since the early days of history mankind has attempted to elevate himself to a high position where there is no need to acknowledge God. The book of Genesis provides great insight into the start of humanity's journey through the ages, and his propensity toward "going it alone" without God.

In Noah's day, we read:

And God saw that the wickedness of man was great in the earth, and that every imagination of the thoughts of his heart was only evil continually. (Genesis 6:5)

Far from the humanistic philosophies of our day that would say man is inherently good, here the Creator is informing us that the opposite is true. Man is inherently bad; at least man apart from God and His influence.

A few verses later we read:

The end of all flesh is come before Me; for the earth is filled with violence through them ... (Genesis 6:13)

In Romans, the apostle Paul makes the following observations about humanity.

God's indignation is being revealed from heaven on all the irreverence and injustice of men who are retaining the truth in injustice, because <u>that which is known of God is apparent</u> among them, for God manifests it to them. For His invisible attributes are descried from the creation of the world, being apprehended by His achievements, besides His imperceptible power and divinity, for them to be defenseless, because, knowing God, not as God do they glorify or thank Him, but vain were they made in their reasonings, and darkened in their unintelligent heart. (Romans 1:18-22)

In short ...

We can know of God from seeing that which He created. His existence is <u>apparent,</u> and we are defenseless if we fail to acknowledge Him and give thanks to Him for creating the wonders of the universe and for giving us life.

If we read further in Romans 1, Paul goes on to tell us the side effect of mankind's turning away from the Creator. Since man chooses to ignore God and go his own way, God allows him to experience certain consequences ... dishonorable passions (here

14

homosexual behavior is described), a disqualified mind, injustice, wickedness, evil, greed, envy, murder, strife, guile, depravity, the detesting of God, pride, invention of evil, lacking natural affection (Romans 1:24-32). In these words we see an apt description of humanity – at least humanity that ignores God – in our present day.

So it's a bit like "Lord of the Flies" when man tries to live apart from God and His *blueprint* – His design for this universe. When God created, He built a certain design into the created order. Natural laws such as gravity are examples of this design. Recognizing God we should seek to be in harmony with that design; listening closely to His instructions ... the things He approves of and the things He does not.

In our less-than-perfect state we may have certain impulses or desires that are counter to God's design, but we should not be guided by a base "if it feels good do it" approach to life. If we would live in harmony with God's created order, I suspect the world would look much different from the rebellious lot we see all around us.

The Bible tells us that mankind was created in God's image. Christ's purpose is to bring humanity to the point where we are *fully* in God's image. But we have far to go to reach that pinnacle. In the meantime we live in a world crying out for redemption. And we live in a world where the wickedness of man's heart is clearly seen. Many of our woes result from things that mankind is responsible for. Ignoring God's design and trying to set our own course in contrast to that design leads to many of the problems we see around us.

So, while God the Creator may be invisible in form, His existence is obvious through His creation. Yet mankind has chosen to ignore God and even claim He does not exist. God is not acknowledged or thanked, and instead mankind turns to a different "authority."

They [mankind] change the glory of the incorruptible God into the likeness of an image of a corruptible human being and flying creatures and quadrupeds and reptiles. (Romans 1:23)

15

In Old Testament times man turned away from God the Creator and instead made gods of things that were visible ... things that were tangible ... idols. Man preferred created things rather than the Creator Himself. We may look at this idol worship as something that is archaic and irrelevant in our present day, but let me suggest that what we worship today is human authority (government leaders or humanistic ideals) or "science" (or at times certain brilliant men and women that are behind scientific discovery and theory). We look to them for instruction and even for the salvation of mankind while ignoring the one true God Who created all things.

An interesting and enlightening example can be seen in an episode reported in Genesis.

Tower of Babel

And they said, Go to, let us build us a city and a tower, whose top may reach unto heaven; and let us make us a name, lest we be scattered abroad upon the face of the whole earth. (Genesis 11:4)

The Tower of Babel! Keeping in mind that God had commanded mankind to be fruitful and inhabit the earth, this tower was a direct rebellion against Him. "We will not scatter and inhabit the earth. We will stay in this one place. And behold what we can do on our own, without acknowledging God and without His help." (My summary of the thought-process in quotations.)

This was a world thinking it did not need God, countermanding God's plans and directives. It was the pride of man and *his* abilities apart from God. The ability to build a magnificent tower for the world to see and marvel at!

So God thwarted man's plans, scattering them to distant places and "confusing" their tongue, making it difficult to communicate and to repeat the tower incident.

But with the internet and advances in technology, mankind has regrouped! Today we have a new version of the Tower of Babel that has been built, and the tower is *science*. How marvelous the discoveries mankind has made, and the advances in science and medicine. These discoveries can be good things if they are not a substitute for faith in God and recognition that He is the Creator of all that we see and all that we discover. But sadly this is often not the case. It is "science versus God." It is the advances of science replacing the need for God. Often it is science mocking God and positioning Him as archaic and irrelevant and even mythical. Beliefs based upon the Bible – God's revelation – are ridiculed and set aside in favor of "pure science."

But as already stated, the evidence favoring an intelligent Creator is overwhelming. Science, properly done, will always *include* a recognition that God is behind it all, and that He created these things we are discovering thru science. Science that *begins* with the premise that there is no God and that there was no Creator responsible for creation is *bad science*. This is not objective scientific discovery but begins with a biased premise!

Science is not perfect as many will often claim. For a fair number of years in my life I was told butter was unhealthy, and to substitute margarine instead. This was science at work. Later we were told that butter is not unhealthy after all, and in fact margarine might pose some health risks. (Alas, all those years of suffering thru the distasteful margarine era when I could have been eating butter!) Some will say that science has now evolved and that it can now be believed. But I suspect the same was said when margarine was being touted as a better alternative.

Furthermore, science is sometimes manipulated by those wishing to leave God out of the equation, or by those seeking to use science as the ultimate authority to accomplish their objectives. "Marvel at this amazing tower of science we have built and bow down to every edict declared by the scientific experts without question." But one problem is that experts will often disagree.

There are often motives behind things, so the science being touted may not even be objective science. Could it be that better science is being suppressed by those wanting to secure power, or authority, or money?

As I write these words the world is grappling with a virus pandemic. And as I pause to contemplate the unfolding of events, I see this virus being used as a means to control the masses thru fear of sickness. The virus is certainly real, but I also see it being used as an opportunity by those wishing to exercise greater control over the masses, building power and strengthening authority. Whatever the experts decree, the masses accept; allowing governments to take greater control over the lives of individuals.

I see differing opinions on this virus and its prevention. But dissenting medical opinions are buried by the Press and by authorities intent on presenting only the "official" narrative, thereby keeping fear alive and enabling their preferred political opinion to rise in power. Propagation of fear begets willingness to be controlled, thereby begetting increasing power of government "for the good of the people."

This might all be harmless if the motives of those in power were good. But I suppose the same could have been said as the Tower of Babel was being built. "While God has said to scatter and populate the earth, surely we are better off to congregate in this one place and built the greatest city ever built, for the good of humanity."

Many today belittle religion, saying it is archaic and mythical. And those within religious circles have done much to hurt their credibility, what with division and fighting and failure to earnestly study that which God has revealed before coming to the conclusions they espouse.

But this is not about religious belief versus scientific fact. This is not about religion at all. It's about whether or not God exists – whether or not He created this universe – and whether He incorporated into His blueprint behaviors that are acceptable and in harmony with His created order – in contrast with behaviors that are out of harmony and that are destructive and unsatisfactory; based on the faulty man-made premise that "anything goes."

If God exists, evidence will exist that points to this conclusion. And indeed as

18

we look around us, the evidence is everywhere.

One point before we move on. If there *is* an intelligent Creator responsible for this world, and this universe, and life; then we may assume He has built some meaning and purpose into His design. Anyone that engineers and builds a product does so with a purpose for that product in mind. The building of the product, and in this case the creation of all things, is done to fulfill some purpose. And in using the engineered product its purpose must be considered if it is to function in accord with its intended design. If we determine our own idea for the use of the product, we run the risk of acting contrary to the designer's purpose. And we run the risk of frustration when the product does not serve in accord with our wishes. The meaning and purpose is not up to the user of the product. It is determined by the engineer and builder of the product.

Now – if there *is* an intelligent Creator – and if He wished to communicate with His creation beyond just what we can discern from examining the creation itself – how might He do so? This is the question we will tackle next.

Has God Communicated with Us?

——

Beyond the general evidence of God's existence revealed by the created order, has God chosen to communicate more specifically with us? This would be entirely His choice. If God chose not to communicate with mankind, we could not force Him to do so. We could merely examine the observable evidence and come to certain conclusions about Him. Many today believe this to be the case, and they believe that we can only know of God thru a study of the universe.

But the question is ... has God chosen to communicate with mankind on a more detailed level? Has He chosen to tell us things about Himself, or about the reason for our existence, or about His plan for the universe, or about what lies ahead?

To answer this question we must consider the evidence. God does not stand before us visibly, and He does not speak to us with an audible voice. But is there other evidence to consider, beyond the creation itself, that might tell us of a means used by God to communicate with mankind?

Again, we cannot assume God has chosen to communicate with us at all. He may have chosen not to do so. And so we pull together the evidence that is available to us and we consider it.

What about dreams, visions and God's audible voice?

God could choose to speak to man thru dreams and visions, or thru an audible voice. Some claim that He does! And so a part of the evidence to consider is the testimony of those who claim to have heard from God thru dreams, or visions, or by hearing His voice.

But are those that provide their testimonies being honest, or are they fabricating stories? Or do some honestly believe they have heard from God, not knowing it was their imagination, or a mental illness, or perhaps some supernatural entity other than God?

One problem is that there are many different accounts that often conflict as to the information we are given concerning God. So how can we know which of these accounts is legitimate, if any, and which are not?

If God has chosen to reveal certain things to man, would He do so in a way that could be so confusing and so easily misunderstood, to the point that we can never really be sure what He is saying to us?

What about our conscience?

If God created us, could it be that our conscience is the means thru which He speaks to us? This could be the means He uses to teach us what is right and what is wrong; what is moral and what is immoral; what is ethical and what is unethical.

But here again we have the problem of subjectivity. Each person, speaking from his own conscience, differs greatly from other persons. We can find no consensus as to absolute right and wrong. Furthermore, if some ignore their conscience, will it not become weakened or hardened so it can no longer function as a guide at all?

So once again we ask ... if God has chosen to reveal specific information to us apart from what we can discern by examining His creation, would He use such a means that would be so confusing and unclear?

What about prophets?

Some say God has spoken to the mass of humanity thru certain select men and women ... prophets ... those chosen to take a message directly from God and communicate it to all others. Some say prophets existed in the past, and others say God still uses prophets today. But here, too, there is disagreement, and many conflicting accounts from those claiming to be prophets. And if prophets are, or were, used by God ... we must have a means to discern the true prophets from the false. We must carefully consider the testimonies of those claiming to be prophets.

What about a written record?

Could God have chosen to use men and women to record in writing a message coming directly from Him, and revealing specifics concerning Himself, His purpose for creation, His blueprint for creation, and His plan for what lies ahead?

At this point we will consider the Bible.

Is the Bible How God Has Spoken to Us?

———

At this point allow me to propose a hypothesis. I suggest that the Bible is God's revelation directed to mankind, to provide details concerning His created order. While other writings from antiquity claim to be divine; I believe the evidence clearly points to *the Bible* being God's method of revealing Himself to us. He tells us of His plans, and of His design, and of His will for mankind.

In my lifetime I have lived in Michigan, Florida, and now Kentucky. Most of my friends and family members are Christians. I have always been taught that the Bible is God's Word revealed to mankind. I never had reason to question this, and everyone around me was so definite about the fact that the Bible is clearly God's Word. Every pastor and Bible teacher I ever encountered told me the Bible is the Word of God. Preachers pounded their pulpits and raised high their Bibles while shouting in a loud voice, "This is the Word of the Lord."

And so I can take this torch that has been passed to me and shout in an equally loud voice, "This is the Word of the Lord." I can do so because those that preceded me were so sure about the fact, as were those that preceded them, and so on. We know this is the Word of God because everyone knows that this is so.

But what is the *evidence* in support of this conclusion?

In these days where there are many skeptics demanding to know "why should I believe?" – a presentation of the evidence is needed.

Let's assume that God has chosen to reveal Himself to us thru the written word. This seems like a very good way to preserve the consistency of the message. Once recorded and preserved, it cannot shift or change as could our conscience, or the testimony of prophets, or dreams or visions.

But there is a problem! There are other writings besides the Bible that various people claim are from God. What about the Koran that is cherished by Mohammedanism? Brahmanism and its Vedas? Buddhism and its Tripitaka? Or the Book of Mormon? What about the many others also claiming such authority?

Does it have to do with our culture? Most of those around me teach that the Bible is the Word of God. But what about those raised in Iran who are taught that the Koran is the Word of God? What about those born into the Jewish culture where everyone around them is teaching the Torah, but not the writings of the apostles? Has God blessed us with His revelation; the Bible ... while others born into other situations or cultures are being misled?

How do we know other writings claiming Scriptural status are *not* a message from God, as genuine and authentic as the Bible? A scrutiny of all such writings reveals with certainty some major differences, so they cannot *all* be God's voice – else there would be no consistency in the message He is wanting to convey to us.

Furthermore, let us consider the Bible. The Bible consists of 66 books that have been determined to be the Word of God. But other writings were evaluated centuries ago, and they were deemed to be uninspired and not the Word of God. But were the individuals who made these decisions correct? Did they include the correct writings? Did they leave out any? Consider that the Roman Catholic Church accepts some additional books that other Christians do not. Who is right? And consider some well-known figures from the past, like Martin Luther, who would have us remove the book of James from our Bibles if he had his way.

And so we are faced with many different writings that we must consider, and we ask the question ... is this a part of God's revelation to mankind?

But unfortunately most people today are not willing to think too hard or invest time to study the evidence. And some people want to prevent others from looking at the evidence. We are commanded to accept the fact that the Bible; or the Koran; or some other writings are from God, based on the strength of certain teachers and scholars. We do not study or think for ourselves. And if the set of teachers and scholars around us are wrong there is no hope of finding the truth!

Consider the pressure on individuals within the various cultures of our day. If you are a Jew but become a Christian, your family and friends will disown you. If you are a Muslim and become a Christian, you might be executed. If you are a Christian but do not subscribe to what is considered to be "orthodox" beliefs, you might be asked to leave the church.

And so if God has chosen to reveal Himself to us thru the preserved written word, we have many different writings to consider as possible candidates ... and we must consider the possibility that none of them are really God's Word.

Let us consider the situation among Christian believers today. I have often heard the battle cry, "The Bible says it! I believe it! That settles it!" This is the proof that is offered to any who might disagree.

A hundred years ago preachers could proclaim truth from the Bible, and not many would disagree; since most in our culture accepted that the Bible was the Word of God. But our culture today is different. The tide has turned, and no longer does the Bible command the respect it once had. Believers express their opinions on various issues, even quoting from the Bible, but this does not have the impact it once did.

People today are more independent, and less apt to accept a belief simply because others have passed the belief to them. It is not that they are saying, "I will not believe you, no matter what." Instead they are saying, "I will not believe you unless you can prove your point from the evidence." But Christians today are not ready for this challenge. The average Believer today does not

27

know why he believes the things he believes. And if the average person were to really think about why they believe, they would be forced to admit they are basing their beliefs on things that have been taught to them by others without understanding the evidence behind these things being taught.

There is the story of a newly married bride preparing a pot roast for her husband, and she begins by cutting both ends off the roast. When her watchful husband asks why she has done this, she replies that this is just how you prepare a roast, and when pressed further she does not really know why. When the young woman calls her mother to ask why it is that both ends must be cut off from the roast her mother replies, "Because the pan that I always used was small, and I had to cut off the ends to make the roast fit." We often believe what we believe without really knowing why we believe it.

Beware of spreading falsehoods

If we make claims about God to the world based on the Bible, we had better know for certain that the Bible is God's Word and that we are properly understanding it; or we could be spreading falsehoods about Him. We could actually be *opposing* God, all the while thinking we are speaking for Him.

Those of us who believe the Bible is God's Word are familiar with Saul, who later became Paul. Before Paul's Damascus Road experience, he was passionately doing what he believed was God's work. No one could have convinced him that he was on the wrong side, as he physically pulled Christians from their homes to persecute them or to kill them for proclaiming the name of Jesus Christ. Paul was devoted, and zealous, and sincere, and passionate about his beliefs. And he thought we was speaking for God. But he was wrong.

I wonder how many there are in the world today just like Paul prior to his experience on the road to Damascus. False witnesses proclaiming things about God that are not true!

Let us consider the evidence.

Is the Bible a Reliable Historical Record?

——

Let's begin by considering the evidence supporting the reliability of the Bible as it exists today. While this will not prove that the Bible is God's message to mankind, it is an important first step to assure us that the contents of the Bible were reliably passed down to us through the many years since it was originally recorded in writing.

1. Survival and preservation of the Old Testament

The Bible has more manuscript evidence than any of the top pieces of classical literature. The Jewish people preserved it as no other manuscript has ever been preserved. They had special classes of men whose sole duty was to preserve and pass down the documents with almost perfect fidelity.

When making copies of the manuscripts they kept counts of every letter, word, and paragraph. They counted the number of times each letter of the alphabet occurred in each book. They noted the middle letter of the Pentateuch and the middle letter of the entire Hebrew Bible. And they made even more detailed calculations to ensure the accuracy of the copy.

As a result of such stringent safeguards, there is little divergence and change found in manuscripts produced centuries apart.

When the Dead Sea Scrolls were discovered in 1947 it became possible to reconstruct more than 500 books. Included were copies of the Old Testament text dating from over a century before the birth of Christ. The Scrolls demonstrated the precise accuracy of the copies of the Old Testament over a thousand-year period.

The Old Testament is the oldest written recording of history still in existence. The table of nations found in the Old Testament is remarkable in its accuracy.

All this despite severe persecution through time where many have tried to burn and ban the ancient texts.

2. Later validations of the Old Testament

The Septuagint was the Greek translation of the Hebrew Old Testament, created 285-246 B.C. It was based on a Hebrew text 1000 years older than any existing Hebrew manuscript, and bears witness to the accuracy of the Old Testament text.

Origen's "Hexapla" was created in the second century and also bears witness to the Old Testament's accuracy.

Other witnesses to the genuineness of the Old Testament text include the Samaritan Pentateuch, the Aramaic Targums (A.D. 500), the Mishnah (A.D. 200), the Gemara (Palestinian A.D. 200, Babylonian A.D. 500), and the Midrash (100 B.C. – A.D. 300). These consisted of commentaries and teachings that included portions of the texts.

3. Survival and preservation of the New Testament

The New Testament writings were the most frequently copied and widely circulated books of antiquity. There remains over 5,600 known Greek manuscripts today. No other document of antiquity comes close.

In "The Case for Christ," Lee Strobel speaks of his interview with noted scholar Bruce Metzger. Following are a few notes from that interview beginning at page 75 of Strobel's book.

"What the New Testament has in its favor, especially when compared with other ancient writings, is the unprecedented multiplicity of copies that have survived."

"The more often you have copies that agree with each other, especially if they emerge from different geographical areas, the more you can cross-check them to figure out what the original document was like."

"We have copies commencing with a couple of generations from the writing of the originals."

"We also have translations of the gospels into other languages at a relatively early time."

Metzger's conclusion (page 82), "The last foundation for any doubt that the scriptures have come down to us substantially as they were written has now been removed."

Strobel also quotes noted scholar F. F. Bruce (page 82) who stated, "There is no body of ancient literature in the world which enjoys such a wealth of good textual attestation as the New Testament."

While there are no known existing *original* manuscripts of the Bible, the great abundance of copies makes it possible to reconstruct the original with almost complete accuracy.

4. Testimony of extra-biblical writers

There are many writers outside the Christian community that provide evidence of the Bible's accurate transmission through the ages. To mention a few – the Prologue to Ecclesiasticus (130 B.C.), Philo (40 A.D.), and Josephus (end of the first century A.D.). Josephus notes that the Jews esteem the writings as containing divine doctrines, and to persist in them, and if necessary to die for them.

In "The Case for Christ", author Lee Strobel notes that we have important references to Jesus in Josephus (an important Jewish historian in the first century) and Tacitus. In Strobel's interview with scholar Edwin Yamauchi, the latter states (page 107), "Tacitus recorded what is probably the most important reference to Jesus outside the New Testament. In AD 115 he explicitly states that Nero persecuted the Christians as scapegoats to divert suspicion away from himself for the great fire that had devastated Rome in AD 64."

Yamauchi goes on to note the significance of the writings of Tacitus (page 108). "This is an important testimony by an unsympathetic witness to the success and spread of Christianity, based on a historical figure – Jesus – who was crucified under Pontius Pilate."

5. Archeology

No artifact discovered by archeologists has contradicted any statement within the Bible. And discovery after discovery has established the accuracy of many Biblical details, including the historicity of Old Testament traditions.

Archeology cannot prove that the Bible is God's revelation to mankind, but it can prove the historical accuracy of events as recorded in the Bible. Furthermore, archeology has, at times, shed light on the meaning of some biblical passages that had puzzled interpreters before certain discoveries were made. The finds display that biblical accounts match up with objective facts from the ancient world, establishing the general reliability of the Bible as a historical record.

Archeology can also help to supplement information not dealt with directly in the Bible, providing background and context to help one's understanding. For example, understanding an area's topography gives us a better picture of how and why things played out in a battle that may have been described.

Archeology has helped to establish the Bible as a reliable document, as reliable as other historical records such as the works of Josephus or the accounts of Julius Caesar.

Josh McDowell includes *many* detailed examples of archeology confirming the Biblical account of history in his encyclopedic work, "The New Evidence that Demands a Verdict." I would also recommend "Why I Believe" by D. James Kennedy that also provides some great specific examples. And one additional work I'll mention that offers many details concerning archeology (along with many other great points concerning the legitimacy of the Bible) is "Know Why You Believe" by Paul Little. Where the McDowell book is encyclopedic in nature and therefore not easy to read, Little provides his arguments in a very easy-to-read fashion.

6. Languages

Concerning the Tower of Babel account from the Bible, there is considerable evidence that the world once had a single language. Sumerian literature notes this fact several times. Linguists have found this theory helpful as they categorize different languages.

7. Fulfilled prophecy

A host of prophecies that were fulfilled support the legitimacy and accuracy of the Bible.

Many Old Testament prophecies were fulfilled throughout history and substantiated by secular historians and archeological finds. And many Old Testament prophecies were very *specifically* fulfilled by events in the life of Jesus Christ and recorded in the New Testament.

Again, many detailed examples are offered in McDowell's book.

8. Diversity and unity of the Bible

The Bible is diverse in terms of the number of different authors that contributed, and the many different literary styles used, yet it shows unity and continuity. It was written over a period of 1400 years, in different lands, by people from diverse walks of life, and employing a wide variety of literary styles. But it is clearly one book telling one story; the story of mankind – a mankind that God created and that He is now telling us about.

Summary

So the evidence supports the Bible as a credible, historical record, and the manuscripts available to us today are faithful to the originals.

But is the Bible *more* than just a historical record? Is it God's message to mankind?

Is the Bible God's Message to Mankind?

———

Regardless of how faithfully the Bible was preserved through the ages in a reliable form, we are still faced with the question – is the Bible God's message to mankind, supernaturally created with the purpose of providing information to us concerning God and His desires and plans for mankind?

What about other writings that claim to be inspired by God?

To thoroughly consider all writings that could perhaps be inspired by God – His communication to mankind – we would need to assemble all of the possible manuscripts and study them, looking for and contemplating the evidence. This would be an arduous task, since many of the manuscripts would be hard to find and possibly corrupted since the originals were first written, and since we would need to have knowledge of a number of different languages to properly study them.

But if we do not undertake this task, how can we really weigh all of the evidence to know what is, and what is not, God's Word?

Without studying in detail each of the various writings that have been raised as a possible candidate, let's consider the basic message being conveyed by each. When we do so we will find a clear uniqueness in the Bible and a wisdom higher than any human wisdom; much different than any other writing claiming scriptural authority.

Consider the explanation found in the Bible concerning the imperfect state of mankind, and our destiny.

God creates all things, including mankind. Man has a close fellowship with God, until man sins and death is the result. Humanity inherits this death condition – mortality – which is accompanied by inherent weakness and a propensity toward sin.

To communicate, God speaks not to the mass of humanity with an audible voice, but to select individuals that He chooses to be His agents. Signs and wonders validate their message to enable mankind to differentiate between the true prophets and those that are false.

God communicates His just requirements to mankind, but time and again mankind fails to be obedient. Experience proves that *none* have the ability to be righteous according to God's standards. All appears to be lost.

God never chooses a select person or group exclusively because they are better than the rest. God's purpose is always to bless *all* of mankind. (This is stated repeatedly in Genesis.) But His means for doing so is to work thru certain select individuals who are called to be His agents. Abraham, Isaac and Jacob were chosen, and God communicated directly with them. But always, the Bible tells us, God's intent is to bless all mankind.

Jacob is renamed Israel, and his descendants become the *nation* of Israel. Thru Moses the Law is given to the Israelites. Always God desires to bless all mankind, but His chosen instrument; the nation of Israel; fails to be faithful. So Israel is removed from her land, and the line of kings ends as the nation is in exile. But even then God speaks thru His prophets of a time when Israel would be restored to her land, and when the Anointed One would come and reign upon the throne.

After years of silence John the Baptist comes bearing the message that the kingdom is near and it is time to repent and get ready. Jesus follows with the same message; the kingdom is near. Here was the Anointed One, ready to fulfill the words of the prophets by sitting upon the throne to reign, and thru Israel all peoples upon the earth would at last be blessed.

But Israel does not recognize the time of the king's "visitation." The kingdom is rejected, and the king is crucified.

The apostles continue to proclaim the coming kingdom message *to the nation of Israel*. Peter calls upon Israel to repent so that the "times of restoration" that were spoken of by the prophets could come, and so that the Anointed One would return. But again Israel rejects the message and persecutes those who proclaim it.

Since the day God told Abraham, "All peoples of the earth will be blessed through you," God has been working thru His chosen agents to accomplish this very purpose. But His chosen agents have not cooperated. It appears that God's plan is at an impasse. How can the kingdom come upon the earth, and how can God bless all peoples thru Israel, when Israel herself continues to reject the message from God?

But we learn that this too is a part of God's plan. This rejection may not have been prophesied before, but it fits right into God's plan for the ages. Israel rejects the kingdom, so God now turns directly to the Gentiles. Paul is not one of the select twelve apostles; but he is an apostle chosen by God nonetheless. He is an apostle of a different kind, and he did not simply proclaim the same message that had been borne by the others who preceded him. When Paul became a believer he did not study under the other believers. This might have seemed like a good idea in the ways of man, but God had different plans; and He revealed *new* things directly to Paul; things that had not been revealed to mankind ever before.

Today God is no longer working thru Israel. He now goes directly to Gentiles, who are joint heirs (equals) with Israel. The focus is no longer on Israel being born again, but on an entirely *new creation*. No longer is the focus on the nearness of the kingdom to come upon the earth; but upon God's *broader* kingdom overarching the entire universe. No longer do we wait for the Lord to come to reign upon the earth; we wait for Him to call us to meet Him in the air – to serve Him in the celestial realm.

But God has not rejected Israel forever. Israel will still serve a purpose when Christ prepares to return to establish the kingdom upon the earth. But for now Israel has been temporarily set aside as God works thru a new instrument; an instrument that had not been mentioned by the prophets of old; the Body of Christ. This plan had been God's *secret* that He kept concealed until the time was right – when it was revealed to the apostle Paul. And this new instrument, the Body of Christ, would be the example of God's *grace* to the entire universe. This was the next step in God's unfolding plan, not previously revealed – until Paul came along.

The day will come when Christ descends, when the trumpet sounds, and when the Body of Christ is called to be with Him to play a part in the heavens. And the day will come when Christ returns to reign upon the earth, when again Israel will play a part. And the day will come when all of God's creation will be subjected to Him, under the reign of Christ, when all are reconciled to God; when not one sheep remains lost; when even death and evil are defeated; when all are saved; and when God becomes All in all.

It all began with God alone, in perfection. Then He created. And now mankind is on a journey, guided by the sovereign God, toward a perfect conclusion.

When we step back and consider this revelation, can any dispute the wisdom and love and power that is displayed?

Just as God's fingerprint is upon His visible creation, letting us know that He does exist and He did create all that we see around us, so also God's fingerprint is upon the Bible – His message to mankind – when we consider the wisdom, the genius and the perfection of the message.

When we consider the other writings that some claim are from God, we know enough of the message being conveyed to see that there is not the same wisdom and perfection that permeates the Bible. God's fingerprint is missing! In no other case do we see the perfection of God, the flaws of mankind, and the perfect plan where not just some; but *all* of creation is reconciled to God, ending in perfection.

And so – consider the perfection of the message being conveyed, a perfection we would expect if the communication has truly come from God.

Consider the Bible's unity.

As we consider the Bible's message, culminating with total reconciliation and perfection, we note the unity found throughout. Despite the fact that many different human agents were at work in relaying God's message to us, and despite the fact that the various accounts were penned at different times over the course of many years, there is a wonderful unity that exists when we consider the account as a whole. Each chapter and verse exist with purpose and helps to form the unified whole.

In "God's Eonian Purpose" by Adlai Loudy we read,

> *"Thirty-three men, chosen by God from various walks of life, 'carried on by holy spirit,' spoke and recorded the revelation He wished mankind to know, during a period of about 1500 years, from about 1400 B.C. to about 100 A.D."* (page 20)

Mr. Loudy goes on to observe the diversity of human agents involved; kings, statesmen, priests, a man learned in the wisdom of Egypt, a herdsman, a tax collector, fishermen, a physician, and seers. Loudy challenges us to consider – "Imagine, for example, another collection of writings compiled in a similar manner … What unity and accord would there be?" (page 21)

Consider the Bible's divine order.

There is a divine order found in the Bible, a progressive unfolding of truth. The judges knew more than the patriarchs; the prophets knew more than the judges. God unfolded the message by many portions and many modes as the time and occasion demanded. ("God's Eonian Purpose," page 22).

Consider prophecy.

Look at the many prophecies found in Scripture that have been fulfilled to the last detail! In "God's Eonian Purpose," Mr. Adlai Loudy observes:

"... twenty five specific predictions were made by the Hebrew prophets, bearing on the betrayal, trial, death, and burial of Christ. These were uttered by different prophets during a period of five hundred years ... yet they were all fulfilled in twenty four hours in one person – the Christ of Whom they spoke." (p 27)

Most of the prophecies recorded in the Bible are not general or vague as is most often the case with many who have made prophecies in the secular realm. Those found in the Bible are specific and with great detail.

In his book, "Why I Believe," D. James Kennedy notes that there are 2,000 specific, predictive prophecies in the Old Testament alone. He includes many great examples.

Would man have recorded his history in this way?

As we consider the story of mankind as found in the Bible we must ask the question; would man have told the story in this way if left to himself? Even the greatest of men is shown to be fallible and sinful. Even those who preceded Christ in His geneology are filled with flaws.

Returning once again to "God's Eonian Purpose" Adlai Loudy states,

"It is quite clear from the character of the Scriptures that they are not the work of man, for man could not have written them if he would, and would not have written them if he could. Why do I make such a statement? Because the Scriptures detail with scathing and unsparing severity the sins of the greatest men,

40

like Abraham, Jacob, Moses, David, and Solomon, charging them with falsehood, treachery, pride, adultery, cowardice, murder, and gross licentiousness. They present the history of the sons of Israel – the chosen people of Jehovah – as a humiliating record of ingratitude, idolatry, unbelief, and rebellion. Therefore, it is safe to say, that the Hebrews, unguided and undirected by the spirit of God, never would have chronicled the sinful history of their nation and its greatest men." (page 12)

The blatantly honest manner in which mankind is described is evidence that the hand of God was at work in this record.

But does the Bible contain the correct 66 books?

We still have the problem that fallible men made the selection as to what to include and what not to include in the Bible, and we are placing faith in them as to these decisions.

I recommend a most excellent book, "The Original Bible Restored" by Ernest Martin. Martin provides evidence that the Bible was "canonized" (approval of which books to include) by the apostles themselves, long before the church councils. The Old Testament canonization process began with Hezekiah when Judah was in danger of being destroyed, and then finalized by Ezra. Both used a "signature" consisting of certain Hebrew letters or phrases to confirm the legitimate writings to include.

Because Ezra was facing a proliferation of false religious beliefs and customs caused by intermarriage, he selected the books to be included in the Old Testament canon, and he arranged them in proper order. Interestingly, he canonized 22 books. These are the same exact writings we have in our Old Testaments today; but with some books being divided at a later time (e.g. Joshua and Judges which were a single book in Ezra's canon). The significance of 22 books? In Hebrew acrostics (a form of poetry) there were always 22 sentences, one for each letter in the Hebrew alphabet. And so 22 would be a sign of completion.

Turning now to the New Testament, the later writings of the apostles talk of a growing turning away from the truth, and this seems to have been their motivation for *sealing* the legitimate writings for the benefit of believers after their deaths. John reported that rebels had infiltrated the church (1 John 2:18,19) and that many were no longer listening to or submitting to the original apostles. (1 John 4:6) Some elders within the church were rejecting John's authority. (3 John 9,10) Peter writes that destructive sects would soon rise from within the church, even denying Christ's return. (2 Peter 2:1,2,13; 3:3,4) He describes an apostasy from the truth and warns against the coming errors. (2 Peter 3:17) Peter said there would be false teachers (2 Peter 2:1) and that many would follow them. When Jude later wrote his letter, these things had already begun.

It is also clear that Paul's primary desire was that sound doctrine be preserved following his death, as he knew there would be a great falling away from the truth, a falling away that had already begun in his lifetime. (2 Timothy 4:1-8) When Paul summoned Timothy and Mark to Rome with the scrolls and vellums (probably certain specific writings), this was probably a part of the canonization process. With Mark being a close associate of Peter's, Martin contends that Paul probably used this occasion to send his inspired writings to Peter for inclusion in the canon – knowing that his death was near.

Luke reported that many were composing "gospels" (Luke 1:1) and since these were being written in a time of growing rebellion, how could one be certain these gospels were accurate accounts?

So recognizing that Christ's return was not imminent as they once thought and seeing the growth of false doctrines and a general turning away from the truth, the apostles began to see the need to preserve the truth for future generations. There needed to be an official written document finalized before their deaths.

Think about this. Seeing the need to preserve truth, and observing the falling away from truth as their lives and ministries moved toward the end, would it make sense that the apostles would simply die and let others formulate the official canon? If they couldn't trust the fidelity of many in their midst even as they lived, how could they depend on the church at a future time to preserve the written truth?

One final note from Martin's book. When we consider the 22 books in the original Old Testament canon and the 27 books in the New Testament canon, we have 49 books in total ... 7 times 7 which represents completion and perfection. This would seem to be a validation of the legitimacy of the canon. It is a shame that this validation has been hidden by the tampering of the later church, as they brought the number to 66 books. Yes, the contents are the same in either case, but the stamp of completion and perfection is clouded when moving from 49 to 66 books.

I have included here just a brief snapshot of some of Martin's key points in "The Original Bible Restored," and I would highly recommend that the reader seek out a copy of this excellent book to read in full.

The writings of E. W, Bullinger and A. E. Knoch

In the extensive writings of both Bullinger and Knoch, who worked independently of one another, we are provided with very detailed outlines of the Bible that show great symmetry and perfection in the text. The writings of both can be easily found. Of special interest is "The Companion Bible" which was compiled by Mr. Bullinger and which contains many of his notes and "skeletal outlines" of each book in the Bible.

As the overall message being conveyed by the Bible shows great wisdom and perfection, so also does a literary analysis of the writings themselves.

Additional writings?

Were there additional writings that might be inspired by God but left out? Again pointing to the perfection of what we have with us today in the books known as the Bible, it would seem that the complete account has been preserved for us.

Furthermore, we read in Colossians 1:25 that Paul *completed* the Word of God. So any subsequent writings could *not* be inspired

Scripture, for Scripture had by that point been completed. This completion was necessary to safeguard God's truth against those that came after the death of the apostles, introducing and propagating falsehoods that would have caused truth to be lost forever.

Different translations and interpretations

Everything I have stated thus far is dependent on our having an accurate translation from the original languages, and an accurate interpretation of what the Bible is teaching.

Unfortunately, the issue becomes clouded by the many different Bible translations today which are focused more on being easy to read than being faithful to the original manuscripts. These translations differ from one another, and they make certain passages appear to contradict other passages.

Coupled with this is the problem of interpretation. Today we have many different denominations, and many different preachers, scholars, teachers and writers ... and while they all start with the same Bible, they teach many drastically different things, contradicting one another. This confusion makes it appear that the Bible is not the Word of God, because supposedly learned men cannot agree what it says.

The perfection of the message is lost when we rely upon the imperfect teachings of men as to what the Bible says. Far from the perfection that is revealed in God's Word, we hear instead of a God Who loves the world (all mankind) but Who is willing to torment some forever and ever. We hear of a God Who says on the one hand that He will seek the single lost sheep until it is found, while also saying that some of the lost will remain lost forever and ever. We hear of a God who will deal with a man who commits a finite amount of sin in this short lifetime by tormenting him with an infinite punishment, forever and ever.

Many believers today proclaim an imperfect and illogical message, and as a result many do not believe the Bible can possibly be God's Word. But it is not God's Word that is the problem; it is the traditions and teachings of men that have crept into the English translation of the Bible, and the many divergent and contradictory teachings being proclaimed today.

Many today teach, supposedly from God's Word,

That God created all things,

That God is in control of all things,

That God is love,

That God created man and placed him upon this earth, which is filled with temptation and evil,

That God sent His Son to die for the sins of man ...

BUT

In the end some will accept Him, and some will reject Him,

And the story will end with a lake of fire tormenting many forever and ever,

While those that *believed* in their short lifetime will spend eternity in heaven enjoying their reward.

A perfect God with an imperfect plan that cannot or will not reconcile ALL, but only some. Even if we try to pin the blame on man for failing to believe; the fact is that God could not develop a plan that would ultimately reconcile all of His creation to Himself, even though that is His desire. (1 Timothy 2:4)

It is easy to see how this prevailing message of Christianity today leads many to the conclusion that the Bible is *not* the Word of God. Preachers talk about man's temporal life of sin repaid with eternal torment, effectively smothering the fingerprint of an all-wise, all-powerful, all-loving God when we examine His Word through most popular Bible translations – and make it difficult to see the perfection in God's Word.

But when carefully and consistently translated, and when carefully and thoughtfully studied and contemplated; apart from the biased teachings of man; we cannot fail to appreciate the wisdom of God as revealed in His revelation to man.

But can the majority of believers be so wrong?

Some will counter by asking how such a minority viewpoint can be correct, when nearly the entire church in all of its denominations teaches of an eternal hell.

My response would be to point to the Bible itself, and to ask when the truth was ever in the majority. When the Old Testament prophets spoke, were they in the majority? When John the Baptist spoke, was he in the majority? When Jesus went up against the Pharisees, was He in the majority? And even at the end of Paul's ministry, when he arrived in Jerusalem and was arrested to be taken to Rome, he was in the minority. Paul was opposed not just by the unbelieving Jews, but also by those who believed but who were zealous for the law and who objected to his teachings concerning grace. (Acts 21:20)

In all of Scripture, when was the majority correct? Today we hear believers marvel that this huge, worldwide church has grown from such a small number of persecuted believers in that early church we read about in the Book of Acts. But as the church has grown, and as "orthodoxy" was defined by the church fathers in the 5th century; what makes us think that the majority opinion concerning the Bible's interpretation is correct?

Is it possible to study God's Word objectively today?

Some will fatalistically declare that even if the ultimate salvation of all is true, it is impossible for the average person today to see this in their study of the Scriptures.

But if one is willing to accept the fact that the majority opinion of the church, commonly referred to as "orthodoxy," *could* perhaps be incorrect, and if he is willing to study the Word of God for himself; then God's plan to ultimately save all of mankind is *clear* and *obvious*. What prevents this from happening is the fact that most have been "indoctrinated" into a system of beliefs that is prevalent in their church, denomination, or circle of friends; and the Bible is studied in light of that context, instead of objectively.

In other words, opinions are already determined before Bible study begins, and the Bible is simply used to prove that the pre-determined opinions are correct. Most begin from the perspective that there is an eternal hell, a place of endless torment, and this viewpoint is then "proven" from the Bible, while setting aside or limiting passages that seem to contradict the viewpoint.

I wish to express my sincere appreciation for the work of Mr. A. E. Knoch and the others that were associated with him. I am not a follower of Mr. Knoch as others might follow Luther or Calvin or Wesley. If I led others to follow Mr. Knoch, I would be no different than those who are dependent upon the teachings of a certain man.

But I will point to the *method* used by Mr. Knoch and say that this method is the best approach for translating Scripture, casting off the biases of mankind as much as is humanly possible, to produce a literal and consistent translation from the original languages. And the end product enables us to study the Scriptures objectively and thoroughly, without need to learn the original languages.

The Concordant Method

Think about this! If God wanted to reveal Himself, along with details concerning His plans for mankind and for His entire creation, how would He have done so?

Would he do so by ensuring that His Word was recorded in a consistent and clear manner, or would He allow the individual men who recorded His message to do so in an inconsistent manner?

Again quoting from "God's Eonian Purpose" by Mr. Loudy:

> *"... thought can only be expressed in words, and those words must express the exact thought of the speaker, otherwise, his exact thought is not expressed."* (p 24)

As the Bible itself instructs ...

47

"Have a pattern of sound words which you hear from me" (2 Timothy 1:13).

Now if the Bible is to relay the thoughts God has wanted to express, then the writers chosen by God must be given the precise words to write, lest there be confusion in the message. This is confirmed by the Scriptures themselves, as in 2 Peter 1:21,

> *"For prophecy was not at any time carried on by the will of man, but holy men of God speak, being carried on by holy spirit."*

If God was not clear and consistent in His message, how would we know today what He was trying to tell us? The fact is that if we will *carefully* study God's Word, we will marvel at its consistency.

I do not use the Concordant Version of the Bible simply because I think it is a better translation than any other. This would be basing my choice on personal preference, much like someone would choose the Living Bible versus the NIV versus the New King James, and so on. I use the Concordant Version because of the *method* that was used.

Look at almost any other translation and you see great inconsistency. A single word, like aion, is sometimes translated *eternal*, sometimes *age*, sometimes *world*. Would God have His chosen writers pass His Word to us so inconsistently? The problem is the bias of man that has crept in. If the translator, based on his understanding of the Bible as taught to him, thinks the word *world* fits better in one particular context because the word *eternal* won't fit; he makes this decision. And all who study from his Bible translation are now affected by this decision.

Or consider the example of *hell*. Here we have a Hebrew word *(sheol)* and three totally different Greek words *(hades, gehenna, tartarus)* and all are simply mixed together indiscriminately into a single English word *hell*. But even more inconsistent are those cases when one of these words, like *hades* or *sheol,* is found and which cannot possibly mean *hell* as we understand *hell* to be ... so the translator must resort to another word in this case; something like *grave.*

A wise God seeks to reveal Himself to mankind by using sound words so we can understand what He is telling us ... but His message is handled carelessly and inconsistently and is distorted to accommodate the teachings of mankind.

I use the Concordant Version because it is *consistent*, and it enables me to look at any English word in the translation; tracing it to the original Greek word; examining how that *same* Greek word was used in all other instances; and knowing when the original writers were using the same words or different words to express their thoughts.

It is only when we use a translation in our study that has taken such steps to be consistent and transparent, that we can fully observe and appreciate the perfection of God's revelation to mankind.

For more detail concerning the Concordant Version, I highly recommend Chapter 2 of Adlai Loudy's excellent book, "God's Eonian Purpose."

What the Bible claims itself to be

Let's consider what the Bible claims itself to be. First, that it is scripture inspired by God.

"All scripture is inspired by God and is profitable for teaching, for reproof, for correction, and for training in righteousness." (2 Timothy 3:16)

And that the words contained in the Bible came from the Spirit (of God).

"... in words not taught by human wisdom but taught by the Spirit." (1 Corinthians 2:13)

That it came not from "the impulse" of man, but by men who were moved by the Holy Spirit and who consequently spoke from God.

"No prophecy ever came by the impulse of man, but men moved by the Holy Spirit spoke from God." (2 Peter 1:21)

That Paul's writings also came through a direct revelation from Jesus Christ, not by human study or speculation.

"For neither did I accept it from a man, nor was I taught it, but it came through a revelation of Jesus Christ." (Galatians 1:12)

"By revelation the secret is made known to me ... which in other generations is not made known to the sons of humanity as it was now revealed to His holy apostles and prophets ..." (Ephesians 3:3)

So the Bible records that all Scripture is God-breathed or inspired (2 Timothy 3:16). God Himself, through the holy spirit, told men just what to write, so the Scriptures are the very words of God. This was a necessity if the thoughts God intended to express were to be relayed to mankind correctly. The inspired writers chosen by God were told which historical facts to record and which to omit. He guided them to record only those things that would be needed to enlighten mankind concerning His plans and purposes.

This inspiration was carried out through a mysterious process by which God worked through human writers, using their individual personalities and styles, to produce authoritative and inerrant writings. This is not to say the Bibles we have today are inerrant, but only the original manuscripts. But what we have today, through the extreme precautions taken to preserve this Word from God, is very close to the inerrant originals.

The prophets were the voice of God in what they said and in what they wrote. We see this when God commanded Moses to *"write these words"* (Exodus 34:27) and when Isaiah tells us that the Lord instructed him to *"take a large scroll and write on it"* (Isaiah 8:1). Hebrews 1:1-2 tells us that God spoke in various ways at various times by the prophets, and then later by His Son. Peter refers to Paul's writings as Scripture. In Peter 1:21 we are told a bit about God's methodology – *"holy men of God spoke as they were moved by the Holy Spirit."*

Consider that the expressions "The Lord said" or "The Lord spoke, saying" or "Thus saith the Lord" occur over 2000 times in the Old Testament. The prophet Jeremiah said, "And Jehovah said unto me, Lo! I have put my words in thy mouth" (Jeremiah 1:9).

The Lord Jesus Himself considered the Scriptures of His day to be the words of God. *"Man shall not live on bread alone but on every command that proceeds from the mouth of God."* (Matthew 4:4) Throughout His earthly life and ministry Jesus clearly spoke of the Scriptures as having authority that could not be broken.

Repeatedly Jesus displayed an unqualified acceptance of the Scriptures of His day to be a word from God without a doubt – every jot and tittle. In every instance when the Old Testament was taught, He never expressed a doubt that it was true and inspired by God to the very word.

Care must be taken as we interpret what God is saying, as the writers sometimes used figures of speech like parables, allegory, metaphor, simile, and hyperbole. Sometimes things are intended to be taken literally, while other times figuratively (e.g. what it means to be "born again"). Furthermore the Bible was written to common people, not the elite. It therefore uses at times nonscientific language, and if we attempt to take it literally and see scientific language when it was not intended, we become prone to error. And at times the Bible may even appear to be at odds with scientific discovery.

Conclusion

I have told you why I have come to the conclusion that the Bible is the Word of God; and the message I see God relaying to mankind in His Word. Now I ask you to consider the evidence available and to come to your own conclusions. Do not believe these things I have said simply because I believe them, or even because I might sound convincing. And do not think I am wrong simply because of the opinions you have been taught by others through the years that you think to be "experts." Consider the evidence, study, discuss, contemplate, pray, and think for yourself.

Evidence that Jesus is the Son of God

———

No historian has direct access to the past. But the *residue* of the past, the *evidence* of things that really happened and that really existed, are directly accessible to the historian. Archeology is one example, as well as eyewitness accounts passed down through the years.

A critical historian that truly wants to know the happenings from the past would want to examine witness statements and confirm things such as the practice of crucifixion and burial customs from the past. After assembling all available data they would consider all possible explanations for the data. This, then, is the practice to be followed as we examine the historical record that is the Bible.

1. The historicity of Jesus

There are a number of accounts substantiating the historical existence of Jesus, recorded by some that were antagonistic to Christianity and thereby making them especially good witnesses.

Eusebius in his "Ecclesiastical History" reports that Papias, bishop of Heirapolis (A.D. 130) observed that Mark was Peter's interpreter and wrote down *accurately* all that Peter mentioned … in order.

Irenaeus, Bishop of Lyons (A.D. 180) was a disciple of John the Apostle, and wrote that the Gospels rest on firm ground, and that even the heretics themselves bear witness to them.

Josephus (A.D. 37-100) was a prolific Jewish historian, working under Roman authority (and therefore taking care not to offend the Romans). He makes many statements that verify the historical nature of both the Old and New Testaments. He reports the books that were legitimately a part of the canon (those writings recognized as inspired Scripture) and the historical life of Jesus.

Josephus refers to Jesus as "a wise man ... a doer of wonderful works, a teacher ... the Christ. ... He appeared to them alive on the third day." Remembering that Josephus took care not to offend the Romans in most circumstances, his words concerning Jesus are quite impactful.

Others giving accounts that record, from very early dates, the legitimacy of the New Testament as a historical record were ...

Cornelius Tacitus (A.D. 117-138), a respected Roman historian and one of the more accurate historians of the ancient world.

Suetonius, a Roman historian and court official (chief secretary) under Emperor Hadrian.

Thallus (A.D. 52), who wrote a history of the Eastern Mediterranean world.

Pliny the Younger (A.D. 112), Governor of Bithynia.

Lucian of Samosata, a Greek satirist from the second century who spoke scornfully of Christ and His followers. Lucian was one of the church's most vocal critics, but he gives an informative historical account of Jesus and early Christianity.

Mara Bar-Serapion (A.D. 70), a Syrian philosopher.

There were also many Jewish references to Jesus as a historical character, despite the fact that the Jews would have been very antagonistic to Jesus and Christianity. The Jewish witnesses include the Babylonian Talmud.

In short, a broad outline of most of the major facts pertaining to Jesus' life is provided in secular history. And it is worth noting

that the centuries themselves are measured from the birth of
Jesus Christ of Nazareth.

2. Eyewitnesses

The writers of the New Testament recorded events they
witnessed themselves, or accounts of their contemporaries that
were eyewitnesses. Often we read, "We are witnesses of these
things."

1 Corinthians 15 (beginning at verse 5) records an extensive log
of eyewitnesses to Jesus Christ after His resurrection. Cephas
(Peter), the twelve, more than 500 brethren, James. Then Paul
notes that the resurrected Lord appeared to him as well.

Other New Testament writers also note eyewitness accounts.
That of Mary Magdalene (John 20:10-18), other women
(Matthew 28:8-10), Cleopas and another disciples on the road to
Emmaus (Luke 24:13-32), eleven disciples and others (Luke
24:33-49), ten apostles and others but with Thomas not present
(John 20:19-23), Thomas and the other apostles (John 20:26-30),
seven apostles (John 21:1-14), the disciples (Matthew 28:16-20),
and the apostles at Mount of Olives before His ascension (Luke
24:50-52 and Acts 1:4-9).

The ascension is worth further mention. Besides the many
witnesses recording their interactions with Jesus after his
resurrection, there were also eyewitnesses present at His
ascension into heaven.

In his speeches recorded in Acts, Peter references the many
eyewitnesses. *"We are all witnesses to the fact"* (Acts 2:32). *"We
are witnesses of this"* (Acts 3:15). And Paul notes in his Acts
13:31 speech, *"For many days He was seen by those who had
traveled with Him from Galilee to Jerusalem. They are now His
witnesses to our people."*

We accept as truth most historical events based upon eyewitness
accounts from those living at the time, or close to the time, the
events took place. *Any* history is simply knowledge of the past
that is based upon testimony.

3. The change in Jesus followers

Consider the change that took place in Jesus' closest followers. When Jesus was crucified they were discouraged and depressed, and they dispersed.

But then after a very short time they regrouped, and a very profound change had taken place. This change did not affect just one or two individuals – it affected the entire party that had followed Jesus. These were simple people that had been taken aback by the loss of their friend and leader in a very horrific crucifixion. But now something had taken place that energized them.

They became committed to proclaiming a very specific message; that Jesus was resurrected and that He was the Christ. They devoted the remainder of their lives to proclaiming this message, even as they faced extreme hardship and persecution and even death. If even *one* of these individuals was privy to a hoax that had been perpetrated, they would have recanted, and the body of Jesus produced.

While they had been educated to believe the Messiah would be a political leader who would help the Jews escape the Roman domination, they now believed that Jesus, raised from the dead, was the Messiah – the Christ – even as the Roman rule continued.

What could account for this dramatic change? They were *convinced* that they had seen Jesus Christ alive after He had died by crucifixion.

The fact that such a sudden transformation of belief could take place in the years immediately following the life, death, and resurrection of Jesus is something to consider. The disciples were without hope, discouraged and depressed. We must ask what *convinced* them, transforming them instantly from being dejected and without hope to rejuvenation – proclaiming the risen Christ – even if it meant their death.

56

Some might say that Islam and other religions have similar devotion, but often their devotion is tied to political extremism. And what makes the followers of Jesus different is they were not just convinced over time as to a belief system – they *witnessed*, and *immediately* upon witnessing they changed! They became willing to die not because of some extremist indoctrination but because they had seen with their own eyes.

People might be willing to die for their religious beliefs if they sincerely believe they're true; but not if they know their beliefs are false. To change so suddenly would tell us they were *sure* about what they witnessed. The fact that these Christians were willing to suffer great persecution and even death because they believed in the resurrection of Jesus Christ is a powerful witness.

What could account for such transformation short of witnessing the resurrected Jesus?

They had nothing to gain by lying and claiming Christ was resurrected if He was not.

4. The logical argument that was presented

As Peter and the others began to proclaim their testimony concerning the resurrection of Christ, they were required to be prepared for rebuttals from a very learned opposition. A weak, emotional argument never would have stood up to the opposition. The message had to appeal to the intellect, as the Jews were a very logical people. If we read the address made by Stephen just prior to his death, or Peter presenting his case to the assembly that had gathered at the feast of Pentecost, or Paul's speeches delivered at various points – we see a very methodical, logical argument being delivered.

Furthermore, much of this was taking place in Jerusalem – the intellectual center of Judea – where anyone could go and examine the tomb, and where there was a large body of official and authoritative witnesses available to recant the arguments being made – or to produce the body if they could. But far from being successfully countered, the movement grew rapidly. And the best that the intellectual opposition could do was attempting to silence the apostles.

5. The empty tomb and the missing body

It is most compelling that the body of Jesus was never produced. Nor did any of Jesus' followers ever pay homage to the tomb where their friend and leader had been buried. Would there not be even one or two that would find comfort in visiting this place?

Indeed the tomb was empty – else the enemies of this movement that began with His resurrection would have squashed it quickly by simply producing His body. But the empty tomb is a mystery that was never solved, and with the precautions that were taken and the large number of organized opposition this is most interesting.

Closely related to the empty tomb is a question we must consider. "Who moved the stone?" The removal of this heavy stone, with a guard present no less, would be a difficult task. The women visiting the tomb were primarily occupied on their journey with the difficulty that lay ahead in moving the stone.

And if the stone was moved and the body carried away to a new location, it would have had to be done in secret, and then kept a secret for years thereafter.

The account given by the women visiting the tomb is given credibility by its defects that would not have been present if this were simply a story told to fabricate a case. Their terror, their failure to inspect the tomb, and their immediate flight are all telling. If this had simply been an empty tomb, or even one that was still sealed, they may have been prevented from fulfilling their intended mission. But they would not have run off in terror and confusion. Clearly they witnessed something at the empty tomb that was extremely out of the ordinary!

The biggest question to ask in all of this is – what would have been the motivation of taking the body from the tomb, keeping it concealed, and not producing the body at some future time to squash this fast-growing movement that was proclaiming the resurrection? And at what point would they have had their opportunity to accomplish this task in secret, especially considering the need to carry lights and tools with which to work?

In "Who Moved the Stone?" Frank Morison summarizes:

"I am convinced that no body of men or women could persistently and successfully have preached in Jerusalem a doctrine involving the vacancy of that tomb, without the grave itself being physically vacant. The facts were too recent; the tomb too close to that seething center of oriental life. Not all the make-believe in the world could have purchased the utter silence of antiquity or given to the records their impressive unanimity."

6. Effect upon the guards at the tomb

A guard was posted at the tomb to ensure that no one could steal the body and claim Jesus was resurrected. If this were a Roman guard, abandonment of one's post or falling asleep were serious offenses, and any guilty of such infractions would be subject to *severe* punishment – perhaps even death. If, as some contend, this was a guard employed by the priests, there would be every motivation to keep the tomb secure lest any might steal the body and fabricate a resurrection story. And if the guard had fallen asleep, surely the noise associated with the opening of the tomb and removal of the body would have awakened them.

After the events occurring at the burial place, the guards reported that the tomb had been miraculously opened. The confusion and fear in these guards when the stone was rolled from the tomb's entrance, their desertion of post and flight into the city, and their having to explain the missing body – argue strongly in favor of the supernatural opening of the tomb and the resurrection of Jesus.

7. Witness accounts of the resurrection

Looking at the historical record found in the Bible, Luke reports that Jesus showed Himself alive by many infallible proofs. When writing Acts, largely a historical account of events taking place immediately following the death and resurrection of Jesus, Luke notes in the preface that he gathered his information from *eyewitnesses*. And Luke himself was a witness to some of the events he recorded.

From the morning of the resurrection to the ascension of Jesus 40 days later, ten distinct post-resurrection appearances are recorded. The Bible records over 500 witnesses of the resurrection that were still alive at the time – men and women of high ethical standards. This was not a homogeneous group, but quite diverse. It might be easy to cause a small handful of people to be convinced of a delusion, but this group numbered in the hundreds, and quickly convinced thousands based upon their convincing testimony. Many names of those witnessing Jesus after the resurrection are recorded, providing strong historical evidence of the occurrence.

When validating historical events in the secular realm we often seek testimony of eyewitnesses that are still living, deeming their account to provide greater accuracy. The witnesses recorded in the Bible's historical record were living at the time and could validate events in Jesus' life before His death, and his post-resurrection appearances.

Also consider once again that those opposing Jesus were never able to produce His body. The Jewish authorities simply attempted to bribe the Roman guard to report that Jesus' body had been stolen; an admission of the empty tomb. And not long afterwards, as the movement grew rapidly, there were no reported attempts to locate the body of Jesus.

8. The testimony of skeptics

It is one thing to present witnesses that are completely sympathetic to a cause and willing to do whatever it takes to support that cause. It is another matter entirely to take one who opposed, or one who was skeptical and demanded more proof before being convinced.

One important witness is the disciple Thomas, who doubted the resurrection after hearing the reports from his fellow disciples. He insisted upon seeing for Himself and touching Christ before believing. His doubts being satisfied, his testimony becomes even more important than those who never doubted and who believed upon hearing the accounts of others. He demanded hard evidence before believing and based upon that evidence he believed.

Another witness who would have been difficult to convert was James, widely known as the brother of Jesus. Throughout his life he saw Jesus as nothing more than his brother – a mere man – certainly not the Messiah. He thought the claims being made by Jesus were ludicrous. He was continually hostile toward Christ throughout His ministry years.

Yet he suddenly changed and became a vocal leader among the Jewish believers in Jesus Christ, proclaiming that Jesus was the resurrected Christ. He became the dominant figure within the Christian movement in Jerusalem. And he stayed true to the end, ultimately suffering death for his faithfulness to the movement.

What could account for such a change, other than the fact that he saw the risen Christ and became convinced beyond a shadow of doubt.

The information available to us concerning James is not totally dependent upon the Bible. The Jewish historian Josephus, who was not sympathetic to the Christian movement, provides validity to the personage of James.

9. Paul

Perhaps the most interesting and powerful post-resurrection account is that of Saul, who later became known as Paul.

Paul was a very competent Jew, perhaps one of the greatest intellects of all time. And he was a passionate persecutor of any who called themselves Christians. He attempted to suppress the rapidly growing movement by force.

While travelling down the road to Damascus he was struck down and witnessed the post-resurrected Christ. The power of his testimony of this occurrence is found in the radical change he underwent as a result ... transforming him from a vehement persecutor of Christ and His followers to a foremost advocate of Christ.

What could account for such a change in one who was such an intellect, and who had opposed Christ his entire life – until the instant of his experience?

We note also that after Paul's experience, he never expressed a single doubt that caused him to dispute the eyewitness accounts offered by the followers of Jesus, or to search for the body of Jesus.

Summary

The Bible records that God used a variety of ways to communicate with mankind, ordered in a logical progression. He spoke with an audible voice, through angels, through prophets, and through Jesus Christ. And if He introduced Jesus Christ as His Son, with a special commission to bring salvation to a mankind bent upon self-destruction, is it any surprise that we see miracles to accompany that supernatural presence in bodily form?

The evidence that was documented, including the many eyewitness accounts, points to the fact that Jesus was not just a man. He was unique. He was commissioned and empowered by God to serve a key role in the history of mankind. He would accomplish what none that preceded Him could accomplish. He would be God's instrument to bring reconciliation and perfection to a world that had fallen into chaos, largely because mankind had turned away from God.

I strongly encourage the reader to find a copy of "Who Moved the Stone?" by Frank Morison and to read it cover to cover. Don't fear; you will find it captivating and compelling – a most interesting read. While Morison provides many excellent points concerning the evidence supporting the resurrection accounts found in the Bible, what I found *most* compelling was his analysis of these Biblical accounts in total – from an investigative journalist's perspective. You will come away seeing the legitimacy of these accounts as credible historical records.

Problems That Have Clouded the Truth

———

Let's consider some of the problems that prevent many from seeing the truth concerning God's existence and His revelation to mankind.

Miracles

Some discount the Bible because of the miracles that are recorded. But miracles are impossible only if one begins with that assumption. If there is a God so wise and powerful that He *created*, could He not perform *miracles* at times to serve His purposes if He wished to do so?

Some fail to believe in miracles because they have never observed one and find them contrary to all that they've personally experienced. But what if the miracles that occurred in the past served a purpose at that time? What if, before God's written record (the Scriptures) had been finalized for future generations, He used miracles to validate His chosen prophets, or to demonstrate His power over the elements?

From a logical perspective we subject ourselves to a "closed system" if we insist there could NOT be any supernatural events. How can one really perform a critical, open, and honest study of history with such a presupposition? When we read eyewitness accounts of the life of Jesus, including the miracles and the resurrection, how can the reader simply discount these events because of an assumption there could be no miracles or resurrection? On what do we base such an assumption?

Even those who opposed Jesus in His day did not deny the occurrence of miracles. Instead, they attributed the power behind the miracles to Satan, and they attempted to kill Jesus to prevent the people from believing in Him upon witnessing a miracle.

The anti-supernaturalist bases his thinking and his logic on the presupposition that God has not directly intervened in history. But what if this presupposition is wrong?

Millar Burrows from Yale observes, "The excessive skepticism of many liberal theologians stems not from a careful evaluation of the available data, but from an enormous predisposition against the supernatural."

Contradictions

Often individuals will attempt to discredit the Bible by presenting apparent contradictions that supposedly prove its imperfection.

Dr. Gleason Archer was learned in over 30 languages, most of them languages of Old Testament times in the Middle East. He taught for over 30 years at the graduate seminary level in the field of biblical criticism. Dr. Archer writes in the forward to his "Encyclopedia of Bible Difficulties" ...

"As I have dealt with one apparent discrepancy after another and have studied the alleged contradictions between the biblical record and the evidence of linguistics, archeology, or science, my confidence of the trustworthiness of Scripture has been repeatedly verified and strengthened by the discovery that almost every problem in Scripture that has ever been discovered by man, from ancient times until now, has been dealt with in a completely satisfactory manner by the biblical text itself – or else by objective archeological information." ("The New Evidence That Demands a Verdict" by Josh McDowell, pages 45-6.)

Also keep in mind that modern Bible translations may appear to have contradictions, but this stems at times from the

66

inconsistency of the translation. Had the translation been done faithfully, these apparent inconsistencies would be removed.

No one can fully explain *all* apparent Bible difficulties. But it is a mistake to assume that which has not been explained will *never* be explained, especially since, over time, most difficulties have indeed been explained. When a scientist comes upon an anomaly in nature he does not give up further exploration, but seeks to find an explanation – and it is often necessary to be quite patient and persistent until the explanation is found.

A great book that deals with many specific supposed contradictions is "A Defense of the Christian Revelation" by Gilbert West and George Lyttleton. And the McDowell book previously mentioned is also a great source of specifics on this subject.

Literary/Biblical criticism

Some "experts" have focused on the Bible from a strictly literary perspective, seeking to discredit its antiquity, its authorship, and its credibility. They seek to uncover contradictions, historical inaccuracies, and textual errors. But such studies have been done without considering unfolding archeological discoveries that can help to shed light. Biblical criticism is based upon a biased worldview – the critic's own dogmatic presuppositions that fail to consider culture and customs in Biblical lands and in Biblical times. Conclusions are based upon subjective theories regarding Israel, her "probable" development, and the compilation of supposed sources (in their opinion) that resulted in the Bible.

Furthermore, often these literary or Biblical experts begin with the supposition that history has had no direct intervention by a Creator, so all is explained in terms of a natural development.

Creation accounts

Many cultures have a variation of the creation story. Some Bible critics will focus on the similarities, ascribing all creation accounts as myth. But the *differences* between the various accounts is telling, not the similarities. The common assumption that the Hebrew account was a simplified version of the Babylonian account is not supported.

Genesis was not myth (Babylonian or otherwise) made into history. The extrabiblical accounts were history turned into myth. The archeological discoveries of creation accounts at Ebla provide evidence that supports this conclusion.

Similarly, various cultures have an account of the flood. The superficial similarities point to a common historical core from which all accounts stem. And the Genesis account is clearly more realistic.

Refusal to confront immoral behavior

At times we face intellectual doubts developed in order to excuse one's immoral life. Some become hostile to the thought of anything that seems to stand in judgment over them or their behavior. To them it is "anything goes."

But if there is a God that created, and if He created with a particular design or "blueprint" for His creation, could He not also determine behaviors that are harmonious with that design and proper, and behaviors that are in conflict with His design and improper?

Absolute truth

Some will dispute any absolute truth whatsoever. Truth is sometimes confused with what a majority *believes* to be true. Others will contend that what is truth for one may not be truth for another; it is a matter of choice. But *facts* do not become true or false based on our acceptance or denial of them.

Either Abraham Lincoln lived, or he did not live. The truth about his life is not made true or false based on what any of us believes about him. He either lived, or he did not. History is an examination of the evidence, including eyewitness accounts from his contemporaries, to determine the absolute truth.

Even the scientist does not have direct access to all objects of his study but must depend upon the reports and research of others that preceded him. Likewise, while the historian does not have direct access to the past, he does have *evidence* of the past – of the things that existed in the past.

Archeology plays a large part, as well as testimonies of those that lived at the time being studied. It is upon these things that we know Abraham Lincoln once existed, and likewise that Jesus of Nazareth existed – and that the history recorded in the Bible really happened.

Mysticism

Some believe that spiritual things come to us only through our individual intuition and are not subject to logical reasoning or ordinary sensory perception as are material things. Therefore it is concluded that spiritual things are not objective, absolute truths, but are subjective and only true for the individual. Some will go so far as to claim that a thing can be true and false at the same time – that God can be both good and not good, both love and not love.

But if there was a Creator and if He did build certain characteristics into the universe and into our beings, and if He chose to reveal Himself to mankind, then these things would be quite *objective* and could be discerned through an examination of the created order and the written record. If a historical event or if some revealed characteristic concerning God is true, then it cannot also be false. What a chaotic and incomprehensible universe this would be if we could not depend upon objective truth.

Differing interpretations

Differing interpretations make it seem that the Bible is imperfect and that it cannot be the Word of God. But if the Bible *is* God's Word there is only one correct interpretation of any given passage; the simple meaning God intended to convey to us. Any imperfection has to do with how the Bible is interpreted.

And instead of arguing in defense of varying opinions, Bible students should work together to understand the single correct meaning God intended, recognizing the imperfection within any given one of us.

It is fair to say that most Christian believers will agree as to what the Bible *says*. But there is much disagreement as to what the Bible *means*. Hence, we have church divisions, hundreds of denominations, and multitudes of individual churches teaching significantly different things. Arguments abound in Christian circles. In short, there is great confusion as to how the Bible is interpreted today.

God has revealed truth to mankind in His Word, but mankind has confused and distorted that truth because of carelessness, laziness and blindly following the specific church leaders one has chosen to follow.

Often those accepting the Bible as being a revelation from God will disagree with each other. But differences in interpretation do not mean the Bible is not divinely inspired. It simply becomes a matter of seeking to uncover the proper interpretation and meaning for any given part of the Bible.

In some cases a passage may be interpreted *literally* by one and *figuratively* by another, thereby leading to a difference of opinion. When seeking a correct interpretation it is important to remember the Bible incorporates a variety of literary devices, and the context will determine whether a term should be interpreted literally or figuratively. And in any given case God intended to relay a thought that is to be taken *either* literally *or* figuratively. It becomes our challenge to determine which He intended in order to correctly understand what He is communicating to us.

It is also important to remember that in the Bible God revealed Himself *progressively*. For example, at one time He spoke through certain chosen individuals (Abraham, Moses, the prophets), then later through a nation (Israel), and still later through a different people group (Christian believers). In Old

Testament times He guided mankind through Israel and the law. But later Israel was temporarily set aside (see Romans 11:25), and the law was replaced by grace and the Body of Christ was revealed. What pertained to Israel in Old Testament times does not pertain to the Body of Christ or the world at large in the present day.

"Endeavor to present yourself to God qualified, an unashamed worker, correctly cutting the word of truth." (2 Timothy 2:15).

A major problem with Bible interpretation is a failure to *correctly cut* the Scriptures. (In most translations *correctly cut* is translated *rightly divide.)*

We must pay close attention to the context. To whom is God writing? Does the passage pertain directly to us in this present era, or was God working differently in that previous era, and perhaps with a different people group?

It is true that all scripture is inspired by God and is beneficial for teaching, for exposure, for correction, for discipline in righteousness, that the man of God may be equipped, fitted out for every good act (2 Timothy 3:16). But this does not mean that all scripture is speaking directly *to us* in our present-day context.

For example, if God speaks to those of Israel in a past era and context; we cannot force that passage to apply to our present situation. God is always the same, but by His choice and to fulfill His purposes He has chosen to work differently in different eras – *progressively* unfolding His plan.

Rightly dividing God's Word is a divine precept on the same level as all other of God's instructions. If we fail to rightly divide, confusion will reign, and it will not be possible to understand that which God has revealed.

For example, when we read; *Go not into the way of the Gentiles ... but go rather to the lost sheep of Israel* (Matthew 10:5-6); we might think this to be in conflict with other passages that command disciples to go into all the world. But both are words of

71

God and both must be true. We cannot simply discard one and retain the other, and we cannot allow one truth to upset another truth. The only solution is to *rightly divide* the word of God. One passage announces God's plan in one era, and the other shows how God is working at a later time.

Consider the common disagreements among believers, all of whom derive their understandings from the same Bible.

Some believe the kingdom Jesus talks about is heaven. Others believe the kingdom is different from heaven and will actually come upon the earth when Jesus returns.

Some believe when Jesus speaks to Israel, we can apply His words directly to the church of our day, thinking the church has replaced Israel. Others believe it is important to distinguish between things spoken to Israel and things spoken to the church.

People have many differing views of "the unpardonable sin" as found in Matthew 12.

People have differing views as to what happens when we die. Do we go immediately to heaven or hell? Do we go into a sleep state awaiting the resurrection?

People have differing views as to what will happen on the earth, and the order of events, in the end times. Some believe the end time events recorded in Revelation have already taken place.

Some believe we have free will while others believe God has determined the course of events.

Again, most will agree as to what the Bible *says.* But opinions differ as to what the Bible *means,* or how it is to be interpreted. The problem within Christian circles today is the same as with the Pharisees of Jesus' day. The Word of God has been transgressed and invalidated by the traditions of men (Matthew 15:1-9). The Reformation recovered some truth that had been lost, but within several generations the church relapsed and allowed creeds and confessions to replace the Bible.

The real question is this. How do the various parts of the Bible fit together? If we fail to rightly divide as the Bible itself instructs us, we will fail to see God's *progressive revelation* and His *progressive approaches* to working with mankind over time.

Many folks will memorize large portions of the Scriptures. While this is beneficial to a point, let me suggest that it is far more important to understand how all of the pieces of the Bible fit together. It is a mistake, leading to error and confusion, if one reaches into the Scriptures and arbitrarily applies any passage to their present situation. Memorization or instant recall of the Scriptures means nothing if one fails to understand how all of the various portions of Scripture fit into God's overall workings.

This is expressed well in the preface to the 16th century translation of the Bible by Miles Coverdale:

"It shall greatly help ye to understand Scripture if thou mark not only what is spoken or written but: -- to whom, and by whom; with what words, and at what time; where, and to what intent; with what circumstance; considering what goeth before and what followeth."

In short ...

"All Scripture is inspired by God, and is beneficial for teaching" (2 Timothy 3:16)

– BUT –

"Endeavor to present yourself to God qualified, an unashamed worker, correctly cutting the word of truth" (2 Timothy 2:15).

Beware the traditions of the Pharisees (Matthew 15; Mark 7). While directed to the Jewish leaders of Jesus' day, this principle seems to have application with the church leaders of our day. As was the case in Jesus' day, religious leaders have inserted the traditions of men into Bible teachings. And like the average person in the Pharisees' day, churches today are filled with blind followers. Beware!

The Verdict

——

Things concerning God cannot be proven like a mathematical equation. Does God exist? Is the Bible really a revelation from God? Is the Koran a revelation of God? These things cannot be proven or disproven scientifically. Instead we are presented with the evidence, much as a jury is expected to consider evidence as it works toward reaching a verdict.

We are presented with the world and universe that are open to examination. And we are presented with various writings that scholars and others tell us are holy scriptures – revelations from God. Some tell us the Koran is God's revelation. Others say it is the Bible. Some make other claims. Do we base our verdict on the culture in which we live? Those raised in Islamic countries generally reach the verdict that the Koran is the Word of God. Those raised in Christian cultures commonly reach the verdict that the Bible is the Word of God. Some reach no verdict at all, believing that one cannot possibly know for sure. And some believe the verdict has no bearing on their life.

But for those willing to examine the evidence, an informed verdict can be reached. I believe the verdict is clear – the Bible is the Word of God, His revelation to mankind – based upon the evidence.

And let me stress the importance of the Bible not just as a historical record, but for the *implications* of the events recorded. The resurrection of Jesus Christ is most certainly a display of the power of God the Creator – but it is also much more. It is a demonstration of death being overcome. And with Christ being the "firstfruit" (as God tells us in His written word) – this overcoming of death and resurrection is something we, too, will experience. Because of what Christ Jesus accomplished through the power of God, we are being told that death has been overcome – a truth we will all one day experience.

I have presented the evidence at a high level and encourage the reader to dig deeper using some of the resources I have mentioned, as well as others you may find in your search. But do search! The importance of this matter cannot be over emphasized.

In the scheme of things, when measured against eternity, this present life is very short. We tend to become occupied with the material things that surround us – the visible realm. But one day this will pass and all that will matter are eternal things – the invisible realm. And while this realm is invisible it is just as real as the things that are visible.

So set aside time to think about what I've presented in this short work. Dig deeper. Contemplate the wonders of creation, and the Creator that is behind all of this. Contemplate the Scriptures and the perfection they contain; the perfect explanation for the observable creation, for this present life, and for where we are headed. There is no other explanation that stacks up!

If this was a jury trial, the evidence supports the conclusion beyond a reasonable doubt. If this were a scientific theory, we would be forced to admit it is the only theory that adequately explains the creation and life.

God created. This world is a work-in-progress. God is leading all things toward a perfect conclusion – a total reconciliation with Him and with all other created beings.

About the Author

Bob Evely is a self-employed business consultant, offering Sales and Sales Management training as well as general business consulting services. He is a graduate of Oakland University (Rochester, Michigan) and has a Master of Divinity (M.Div.) Degree from Asbury Theological Seminary (Wilmore, Kentucky). For three and a half years Bob served as pastor of the Canton and West Point United Methodist Churches in Salem, Indiana; and for five years he served as pastor of the Open Door Free Methodist Church in Nicholasville, Kentucky. Both were bi-vocational positions, with Bob supporting his family through full time employment.

In May 2002 Bob resigned as pastor of Open Door Free Methodist Church to found Grace Evangel Fellowship, an independent ministry based in Wilmore, Kentucky. His ministry includes writing, speaking, teaching, and corresponding via email.

Bob resides in Wilmore, Kentucky with his wife Jill (since 1975). Originally from the Romeo, Michigan area Bob and Jill have five children: Cris (Jen), Dusty (Sharon), Chad (Molly), Kari (Jason), and Scott (Martha). As of this writing they are blessed with 10 grandchildren (Elinor, Allison, Abby, Lilli, Livy, Annabelle, Alex, Max, Logan, and Bailey).

Jill homeschooled all five children, and for 20 years represented Sonlight Curriculum as a consultant. Besides staying busy as a wife, mother, and grandma, Jill is an accomplished soap maker (PrairieKari.com), pottery maker (LaughingBearPottery.com), and she continues to encourage parents interested in homeschooling their children. She is also blessed to spend much time with her grandchildren, teaching them creative writing, soap making, and other life skills.

The author can be contacted at Grace Evangel Fellowship, P O Box 6, Wilmore, Kentucky 40390; or via email bob@GraceEvangel.org

Other Books by Bob Evely

At the End of the Ages; the Abolition of Hell (2002)

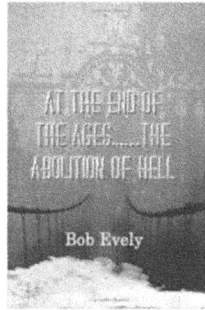

Is hell forever? Most Bible teachers today say that the righteous go to heaven, and the wicked to hell, FOREVER! But is this what the Bible teaches?

"At the End of the Ages" presents evidence that the Bible, in the original languages, reveals that one day ALL mankind will be saved. Through time our Bible translations have become biased through the official teachings of "The Church."

The author argues that teaching about an eternal hell slanders God, and it prevents many from having faith because the arguments in support of an eternal torment are illogical. Would a God of love keep many souls alive forever just to torment them because they failed to "accept Jesus Christ" in this lifetime?

The author shows that the Bible does not teach this. The "lake of fire" is not forever, but only "for the eons," and exists for the purpose of correcting, not tormenting. The purpose of "the eons" (mistranslated "eternity") is to bring ALL mankind to the point where God's authority is recognized, and every knee bows before Him.

Other books taking this position are usually very scholarly and difficult to follow. "At the End of the Ages" is written with the average reader in mind.

The Visitation; An Overview of the New Testament, Part One (2018)

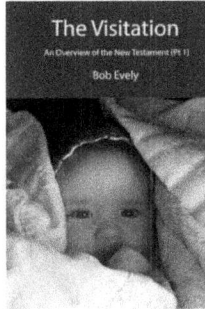

It is important to understand how the various parts of the Bible fit together. It is a mistake, leading to error and confusion, if one reaches into the Scriptures and simply applies any given passage to their present situation. The New Testament can be divided into four distinct parts.

"The Visitation" consists of the four gospel accounts that document the Lord's life and ministry upon the earth.

The Waiting; An Overview of the New Testament, Part Two (2018)

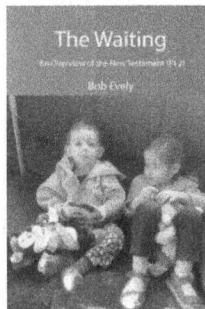

"The Waiting" (or "The Fellowship of Jewish Believers") consists of the first part of Acts and the letters written by the Jewish apostles and leaders to the ecclesia which then consisted of believers among ISRAEL. These believers are encouraged to persevere as they await the return of their king to reign upon the earth in the restored kingdom.

The Pause; An Overview of the New Testament, Part Three (2018)

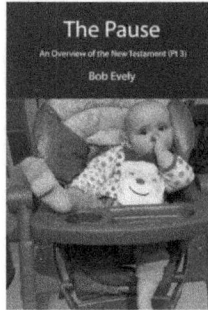

"The Pause" (or "The Fellowship of All Believers") consists of the second portion of Acts and Paul's letters ... especially his later letters that announce "secrets" concealed by God in the past and now revealed. This is a temporary pause in God's working with Israel as he turns to the Body of Christ ... Jew and Gentile alike with no preference.

The Return of the King; An Overview of the New Testament, Part Four (2018)

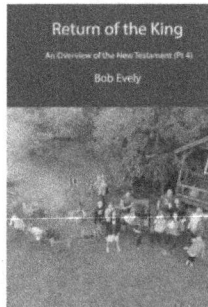

"The Return of the King" (Revelation) records the events leading up to the return of Christ to reign in the restored kingdom upon the earth.

Milestones in the New Testament (2018)

This study is like a walk thru a forest (in this case the Bible). We will stop to observe the most revealing trees along the way; key passages in the Scriptures that set the tone for the Bible as a whole. A more detailed overview of the New Testament can be found in my previous four books.

The Visitation (The Gospels)
The Waiting (Acts Part 1 and the Circumcision Letters)
The Pause (Acts Part 2 and Paul's Letters)
The Return of the King (Revelation)

This present work covers the same ground as all of the above, but in a much more abbreviated fashion. And the format is designed primarily to facilitate discussion.

That is my purpose here ... to facilitate discussion. Each stopping point is followed by a few brief comments; after which I encourage you to think and discuss with others.

Many shorter writings can be found at GraceEvangel.org

www.ingramcontent.com/pod-product-compliance
Lightning Source LLC
Chambersburg PA
CBHW070108070426
42448CB00038B/2215